# GONNA BE SUCCESSFUL

## THE INTERACTIVE STUDENT SUCCESS GUIDE

Darnell Caldwell

Copyright © 2020 Darnell Caldwell

All rights reserved.

ISBN: 9798675034932

# DEDICATION

This book is dedicated to:

Delaya, Dallan, and Dara, my phenomenal children.
My beautiful wife.
My family and friends, especially my mother, one of the strongest women on the planet.
Every young person that struggles with the question: "Can I be successful?"

*Rest in Peace to two of the most influential people in my life:*

<u>My Father</u>
Archie Caldwell Jr.

<u>My Maternal Grandmother</u>
Dorothy Evans

# CONTENTS

Chapter 1: Can I be Successful?   3

Chapter 2: Winning Happens in the Offseason   14

Chapter 3: Wannabes, Gottabes, and Gonnabes   28

Chapter 4: Gonna be Successful   41

Chapter 5: Gifted   53

Chapter 6: Definite Destination   65

Chapter 7: Your Success is in Your Plan   79

Gonna Be Successful Planner   89

Gonna Be Successful 30-Day Challenge   96

Reference Page   114

Meet the Author   115

# CHAPTER 1
# CAN I BE SUCCESSFUL?

Can I be successful? There are millions of young people who have asked and who are asking this very question. Growing up, I asked myself this question often. I wondered, What does success even look like for someone like me? What does success look like for someone growing up in less than ideal circumstances? My parents divorced when I was very young. I attended low-performing schools from kindergarten through high school. Poverty, drugs, and crime plagued my neighborhood. My situation didn't exactly contain the ingredients for success. In fact, my environment made failure almost acceptable.

I recall hearing about the unfavorable outcomes that awaited young black males, often. Stories about the plight of young black men seemed to be everywhere: television, music, local, and national news. It seemed that not a day went by without several news stories about young black men being arrested or killed. Sure. I was a young black male growing up on the "wrong side of the tracks". But I was different, I thought. I made good grades. I stayed out of trouble (most of the time). I was a pretty good athlete. I believed that I was a good kid. Much of the negative commentary that I heard about young black males came from strangers, people that I didn't know personally. Their words got my attention but didn't carry much weight.

Then, in elementary school it became personal. A few friends and I were clowning around in class (I told you that I was well behaved most of the time). My teacher's response to our behavior pierced me to the core. In response to our misbehavior he said that some of us might be dead or in jail by the time that we were 21. I don't know that I fully understood the weight of his words at the time but I do know that his words shook me. His words also gave me more reason to ask myself: "Can I be successful?"

You may find yourself trying to navigate success in a world filled with systems that were not created with your thriving in mind. You may find yourself in an unfavorable environment. Know and understand that your background does not guarantee nor deny you success! Success is more about who you become than where you're from. You may find yourself asking the question, "Can I be successful?" Yes! You can be successful. I believe that success is within the grasp of every young person that is bold enough to reach for it. Will you reach for it? If you answered, yes, this book is for you. Your story is likely not identical to mine. Nevertheless, I want to affirm that you can be successful no matter what your background is or what your challenges are. The obstacles in your life are waiting to be conquered.

What is success? If I were to ask 1,000 people for a definition of success, I'd likely get hundreds of different answers. There are many different views on success. In this book when I refer to success, I am referring to *the maximization of your gift(s) for the accomplishment of your goal(s)*. This definition focuses primarily on your personal development rather than external accomplishments.

I used to believe that success was the attainment of massive amounts of money, prestige, and/or fame. While many highly successful people are wealthy, wealth is not always an indicator of success. Not all successful people are wealthy. Some highly successful people solely desire to impact others and seek no financial gain in return. This person is no less successful than the individual whose success has earned him or her a great deal of wealth.

Regardless of your aim you must take full ownership of your success. Success will not be handed to you. Success is not something that can be handed down from your parents. Success is personal. Success is about you becoming the best version of yourself and deciding that you are "gonna" be successful. But the road to success is not an easy one to travel. In fact, it's a lot easier to settle for just being average. If success was easy to come by everyone would be successful. The road contains many obstacles. One such obstacle is fear.

I remember it like it was yesterday. It was my first roller coaster ride. I was finally tall enough to ride! I was super excited. My uncle Eric and I boarded the Texas Cyclone at Six Flags Astroworld in Houston, TX. The seat locks engaged and my excitement quickly turned into fear. The ride began and I was terrified. The drops were frightening. After the first drop I cringed in fear in anticipation for the next one and the next. The ride was only a couple minutes long, but in the moment, it felt like a lifetime. I was paralyzed by fear. My fear kept me from enjoying the moment that I'd been waiting for! Many people never pursue success because they fear the unknown. They fear that they aren't good enough. They fear what other people might think. Ultimately, they fear failure. Fear is an enemy of success. Failure is part of the process. Every success story is preceded by countless failures. No one likes to fail but the reality is you'll never succeed if you're too afraid to try, fail, and try again. I want to challenge you to face your fears, enjoy the moment, and embrace the process. Don't allow fear to keep you from your success. Don't spend too much time wondering if you have what it takes. I assure you that you have everything that you need. George Washington Carver said, "Start where you are, with what you have. Make something of it and never be satisfied."

The above statement by George Washington Carver is extremely impressive considering that he was born a slave. He lost his mother when he was very young and never met his father, he died before George was born. While he was still a boy the Emancipation Proclamation was signed, abolishing slavery. Still, growing up black was extremely difficult and it was nearly impossible for a black person to get a quality education. Nevertheless, George had an unquenchable desire for it. Unfortunately, there was no school for black people in his hometown of Diamond, Missouri. So, at roughly 12 years old he walked nearly 10 miles to attend school in a town called Neosho.

When Carver left for Neosho, he had no idea where he would live. It was too far to travel back and forth from school to home each day. So, at just 12 years old he had to figure out his own living arrangements. Fatefully, he met Mariah Watkins and lived with her and her family. Carver's thirst for education was lifelong. He went on to become one of the world's greatest scientists. He single handedly gave new life to southern agriculture. At the time, the south relied heavily on cotton production. However, the many years of excessive cotton production had diminished the soil quality.

George Washington Carver developed techniques using peanuts and soybeans to replenish the soil with the needed nutrients. He also went on to create 300 products from peanuts and 118 from sweet potatoes. His skills were desired around the world and could have made him a fortune. Yet, he turned down opportunities that could have made him very wealthy. Instead, he committed himself to his defining work at the Tuskegee Institute.

Before George Washington Carver became one of the world's most sought-after scientists, he had an unstoppable desire for education. He believed that a good education was possible even though the world that he lived in didn't value his education. His desire began in his mind. He didn't let the many obstacles that he faced stand in his way. He believed that he was "gonna" be successful and he did just that. He defied the odds. Likewise, if you are to be successful you must first believe in you. The popular saying, "A mind is a terrible thing to waste", is very true. Your ability to unlock the limitless capabilities of your mind and think beyond your circumstances is critical to your success.

Mankind's ability to think beyond his/her circumstances separates him/her from the rest of creation. Lions are powerful, ferocious, and fearless. They are known as the "King of the Jungle". However, the most that a lion born in the savannas of Africa can ever become is a lion in the savannas of Africa. On the other hand, you have the potential to become as great as you believe you can be. George Washington Carver rose from one of the greatest tragedies in human history, Amercian slavery, to become one of the world's greatest minds. Your ability to rise to greater heights relies heavily on your ability to see beyond where you are currently. If you only see what you see as possibilities for your life, your thinking is too small and you are cheating yourself. You deserve so much more! Unfortunately, life doesn't always give you what you deserve.

You get from life what you become. Take a moment and find a mirror. Stand in front of it and look yourself in the eyes and say, "I'm gonna be successful". Say it again but this time say it like you really mean it, "I'm gonna be successful". Repeat this exercise daily. Repeat it whenever you experience doubt and find yourself asking, "Can I be successful?"

# Let's Think About It

1. Have you ever asked yourself, "Can I be successful?" What caused you to ask this question?

   _____

   _____

   _____

   _____

   _____

   _____

2. What obstacles stand in the way of your success? How can you overcome them?

   _____

   _____

   _____

   _____

   _____

   _____

3. What does success look like for you? How will you know when you're successful?

_____

_____

_____

_____

_____

_____


4. If you had the opportunity to ask George Washington Carver one question, what would you ask him?

_____

_____

_____

_____

_____

_____

5. What is your major takeaway from this chapter? How can you apply it (use it) in your own life?

_____

_____

_____

_____

_____

_____

## Gonnabe Principle #1

*"...success is within the grasp of every young person that is bold enough to reach for it."*

## **Notes**

## CHAPTER 2
## WINNING HAPPENS
## IN THE OFFSEASON

We are La Marque Cougars, WHOOSH! We are La Marque Cougars, WHOOSH! We are La Marque Cougars, WHOOSH! This was the battle cry of hundreds of faithful Cougar fans at La Marque High School football games. I consider myself fortunate to have attended La Marque High School. It was once a Texas High School Football powerhouse. To date LMHS boasts 10 state championship title game appearances and 5 state titles. In La Marque, each new season brought the same expectation, a championship. Anything short of a state championship was considered to be a failed season. The championships, trophies, stories, and victories serve as evidence of the school's dominant past. What's not so evident is what separated those phenomenal teams from their opponents.

At the beginning of each spring semester following Christmas break, returning football players went through a program called bootcamp. Bootcamp was intense, really intense. During bootcamp players were broken up into small groups. Each group rotated through a high energy circuit of workout stations. The stations consisted of strength and agility drills. During boot camp coaches demanded maximum effort and would settle for nothing short of "perfection". Failure to meet these demands led to pushups, lots of pushups, and ultimately led to bootcamp being extended. Bootcamp did not have a specified end date. Boot camp could only end when a "perfect day" of boot camp occurred.

Bootcamp caused some to cry and others to quit or at least consider quitting. Personally, I remember leaving boot camp each day feeling completely exhausted from the day's session. My lunch period was immediately following bootcamp. Normally, lunch was a time of relaxation and a time to connect with friends. However, most days after bootcamp I could barely muster the energy to eat a full meal. I would settle for a drink and a short rest from the terrors of bootcamp. During bootcamp, it felt like the coaches were trying to kill us but in hindsight they were teaching us that winning happens in the off season.

Bootcamp provided a phenomenal physical workout. However, I believe the greatest benefit of boot camp was the mental toughness gained from it. Most people quit when they get tired and buckle under the pressure of fatigue. Boot camp taught us to persevere in the face of adversity and pain. Trust me, boot camp provided participants with lots of pain. We were learning to win when no one was watching. Each time that a player kept going when he felt that he could not was a small victory. Small victories are a big deal! Small victories lead to championships.

The benefits of boot camp were not always immediately evident. In fact, many of the benefits didn't manifest until late in the season, during the playoffs. In the playoffs, you either win or go home. In the later rounds of the playoffs most teams are usually pretty evenly matched in terms of talent. As a result, it takes more than talent to win. Playoff games are often won by the team that outlasts the other mentally. Those dreaded days of boot camp produced a certain type of mental toughness and endurance in the great Cougar teams of the past. The result was great success. Their success on the field was merely a byproduct of their offseason.

The former success of the La Marque High School football program is not unique. In the world of sports, dominant performers and teams almost always have superior off season training schedules. Micheal Jordan, Lebron James, and the late great Kobe Bryant are perfect examples. All three are constantly mentioned in the discussion about the G.O.A.T(Greatest of All Time) of basketball. The world witnessed their domination on the court. Maybe more impressive than their body of work on the court is/was their commitment to improvement through grueling training off the court in the offseason.

After being dominated and eliminated from the NBA playoffs by the Detroit Pistons for three years straight, Michael Jordan was exhausted physically and mentally. Playing against the Pistons was brutal on his body. So, he began weight training. The formerly lanky kid from North Carolina added 15 pounds of muscle in one summer. His new strength and physicality enabled him to finally beat the Pistons and win the first of his six NBA titles. Kobe Bryant took his Mamba mentality into his offseason workouts. Kobe had an unquenchable desire to be his best. He is said to have worked out for 6 hours per day, 6 days per week for 6 months straight in the off season. Lebron James reportedly spends $1.5 million on his body per year. As a result, he has won 4 NBA championships and is looking to add more while continuing to dominate the NBA at age 36.

You may be thinking, "I don't play sports, so none of this applies to me" or "I don't understand what this has to do with me". Let me explain. Winning happens in the off season not only in sports but in life as well. Youth is sort of like the offseason. It is a time when the expectations and demands are fairly low, when compared to adult life. In American culture, youth is far too often seen as a time of irresponsibility. I beg to differ. Youth is not a time that should be wasted. Youth provides a great opportunity for growth, development, and exploration.

Early on in the school career of many students the following question is asked, "What do you want to be when you grow up?" The question seems harmless enough but when asked in isolation the question implies that young people must wait until they're "grown" to become significant. Which begs the question, "When does one become grown enough?" A better question is, "What do you want to become and what can you do now to prepare yourself?" Ask yourself that question right now. What do you want to become and what can you do now to prepare yourself? Take action towards your dreams NOW! You don't have to wait until some unknown time in future when you're "grown" enough. The seeds of greatness are already in you. You already have what it takes to get started.

Spending time outdoors enjoying and observing nature is one of my favorite hobbies. I am particularly fascinated by trees. It's mind blowing to behold how massive some trees become. Some oak trees can grow to over 100 feet. They are big beautiful majestic pieces of nature's canvas. Yet, these giants begin as acorns. They begin small and easy to overlook. With the exception of squirrels and other animals that feed on acorns they are seemingly worthless. However, acorns possess a silent secret inside of them. I like to call it "Oak Tree Potential". Inside of every acorn is the potential to become a massive oak tree. Acorns have greatness on the inside. However, it takes time before it can be seen. If you give an acorn time, water, good soil, and sunlight it'll blow your mind by what it becomes.

You too have greatness on the inside, "Oak Tree Potential". Potential essentially means that you have the ability to be successful in the future. Potential doesn't guarantee that you will be successful. Potential only indicates that you're capable of success. Your youth is a time of growth and a time of becoming. Everything that you need to become what you desire to be is already inside of you. You possess the ability to be massively successful and positively impact the world. But in order to do so you have to prepare. You don't have to know exactly what you want to do with your life at this moment. Start where you are and begin asking yourself questions. What are you passionate about? What brings you the greatest joy? What would you do every day for the rest of your life even if you didn't get paid for it? Find your passion. Start practicing and getting really good at the things that you are most passionate about. Success takes time. Jeff Bezos, founder of Amazon, said, "All overnight success takes about 10 years."

Most of us have heard the saying, "Practice makes perfect." It is true. Successful sport teams use the offseason to determine their strengths and weaknesses. From there the team strategizes to determine how to best use the team's strengths to be successful in the upcoming season. Successful people take advantage of their offseason as well. Are you taking advantage of your offseason? Your youth is one of your greatest advantages, use it before you lose it. You will not magically wake up one day and be great at something. No. You have to practice. There's no better time to start than now.

One of the greatest opportunities that you have right now is access to education. Because education is so easily accessible for most Americans it's easy to overlook how much of a blessing it is. Education is powerful. It has the potential to open doors that would otherwise be closed. As a result, it should be taken seriously and prioritized. For some, the word education may cause you to think solely of your school experience. You know the tests, pop quizzes, favorite teachers, and not so favorite teachers. But education is more than getting good grades in school. Don't get me wrong, good grades are important. Good grades can ensure that you get into good colleges and universities. Good grades can also help you qualify for scholarships that will help you pay for your college education. But education is not just about reading, writing and arithmetic. Education is about becoming a learner. The skills that you pick up in school to help you think deeply and master information are extremely valuable. These skills are not only good for mastering your school work. They can be used for the rest of your life as you navigate your path to success.

It's been said that learners are earners and readers are leaders. Personal development is essential for success. Are you developing yourself in your offseason? Are you learning outside of school? If you're not you should be. We live in the "Information Age". Information about nearly any subject is easily accessible. One of the most underused resources in America is the library. Sad thing is the library is free and most people still don't take advantage of it. Library shelves don't just hold books. They hold a wealth of information about just about any subject that you can think of. In addition, we also have the ability to access information via electronic books, audiobooks, and more. Information about your favorite subjects is readily available. Take advantage.

Here's a challenge. Pick a topic and spend at least 30 minutes per day learning about it for 30 days. Imagine if you were to do this for an entire year. At the end of the year your small investments of time would add up to about 180 hours. That's a really big deal! You can use this method to learn more about subjects that you struggle with in school, ways to pay for college, money, entrepreneurship, and more. Your options are nearly limitless.

What are you interested in? Start with one interest and begin learning more about it. Then, find a mentor that currently works in or that has experience in the area that you are interested in. A mentor is someone that can offer you advice and guidance in your area of interest. Finding a mentor may not be as hard as you think. Even if you don't know anyone directly you can ask family members, teachers, counselors, coaches, and others to help you make connections.

There are more people willing to help you than you currently realize. However, they'll only know to help if you make the effort to ask for help. I've always been amazed by how people respond to motorists that have run out of gas. The individual that gets out of the car and begins pushing the car himself normally gets lots of help. Meanwhile the person who sits in their car pouting gets little to no help. People are willing to help people that are already helping themselves. On the contrary, there seems to be fewer willing helpers in the area for the person waiting for help to come. Take action, seek help, and help will come. If you desire to be an attorney seek out help in finding an attorney to mentor you. Ask about steps that you can take now to begin exploring a career as an attorney. If you desire to be an entrepreneur seek help in finding an entrepreneur who can guide you. Whatever your interest, seek out a mentor, someone with expertise in that area for guidance.

You are not too young. In fact, you're the perfect age to begin taking advantage of your offseason. Your youth is one of the greatest resources that you have. I wrote this book just for you because I believe that the greatest resources that our planet has to offer are not the resources found underground such as precious metals and oil. No. They are found in the hearts and minds of young people. Seize your youth and begin to prepare for your future now. Mikaila Ulmer says, "You can't expect great things to happen if you don't work for them."

When Mikalia Ulmer was just 4 years old she was stung by a bee twice in less than a week. As to be expected she was terrified of bees after her bad experiences. Instead of letting her fear paralyze her she began to research bees. Her research became an overwhelming fascination. Around the same time Mikalia's family encouraged her to begin making products for local business competitions. Her great grandmother shared an old family lemonade recipe with her. Due to her passion for bees she decided to add honey to her recipe. Her lemonade was a hit and "Me and the Bees Lemonade Company" was born. In 2015, while still in elementary school Mikalia appeared on "Shark Tank", a TV show that gives entrepreneurs the opportunity to present their business ideas to a panel of wealthy investors. Following the presentation the panel of investors either choose to invest in the company or not. Mikalia wowed the panel with her business presentation and received a $60,000 investment from "shark" Daymond John to help grow her business. The next year her company received an $11 million deal with Whole Foods to carry her lemonade.

Today, Mikalia is just 15 years old and her lemonade is sold in over 1,500 stores nationwide and that number continues to grow. She donates a portion of her company's profits to help organizations that fight to save honeybees. She is a high school student and "normal" 15 year old who loves spanish, science, and rock climbing. She's also the author of "Bee Fearless, Dream Like a Kid".

Mikalia understood that winning happens in the offseason. You are not too young to begin laying the foundation for your success. You are not too young to discover your purpose. You are not too young to pursue your purpose. And you're definitely not too young to live out your purpose. Your youth is an asset not a handicap. In other words, your youth is one of the most valuable qualities that you have. Take advantage of it because it won't last forever. Champions are born in the offseason when no one is watching. What are you doing in your offseason? Don't let another day slip away. Take action now!

## Let's Think About It

1. What do you want to become? What can you do now to prepare yourself?

_____

_____

_____

_____

_____

2. What are your top 3 interests?

_____

_____

_____

_____

_____

3. Do you have a mentor? If not, make a list of 3 potential mentors. If you need help, seek help identifying a mentor using the advice from this chapter.

_____

_____

_____

_____

_____

4. If you had the opportunity to ask Mikalia Ulmer one question: what would you ask her?

_____

_____

_____

_____

_____

5. What is your major takeaway from this chapter? How can you apply it(use it) in your own life?

_____

_____

_____

_____

_____

_____

## Gonnabe Principle #2
*"Your youth is one of the greatest resources that you have."*

# Notes

# WANNABES
# GOTTABES
# & GONNABES

## CHAPTER 3
## Wannabes, Gottabes, & Gonnabes

One day a man named Mr. Prosper traveled to the City of Average carrying a beautiful golden briefcase. His briefcase was filled with flyers printed on fancy linen paper. Each flyer contained these words at the top: "GET YOUR FREE TICKET to the ISLAND OF SUCCESS". Written below these words was the following invitation: "Learn how to receive your ticket tomorrow at 9 A.M. at the City Square". From sun up to sun down Mr. Prosper walked through the city handing out flyers to everyone that he passed on the street until he had no more.

The next day nearly everyone that received a flyer showed up to the meeting and many brought guests. Chatter and anticipation filled the air while the crowd awaited the mysterious man who had given them the flyer. Most people in the city had heard of the Island of Success but had no idea how to get there. Many questioned whether or not the island even existed. There were many questions about the man and the island.

At 9 A.M. a sharp silence came over the crowd. Mr. Prosper stood on a platform and began to speak. He said, "Ladies and gentleman, I want to thank you for showing up today. I know that many of you may have doubts about the Island of Success. I want to assure you that it is indeed an actual place. However, getting there is not easy. In fact, getting to the Island of Success is extremely difficult." After these words half of the crowd left, mumbling and complaining about how they had wasted their time by coming to the meeting. He then said, "To get to the Island of Success you must travel by boat across the ocean." Another half of the crowd left. One lady yelled, "There are sharks in the ocean, so count me out." Another lady said, "The ocean will ruin my hair". A man in the crowd shouted, "I hate boats, thanks but no thanks!" Mr. Prosper continued talking about the challenges of the journey. As he talked the crowd continued to get smaller and smaller until there were only 10 people remaining. He then stepped down from the platform and said, "If you're still interested in receiving your ticket to the Island of Success, meet me at the dock tomorrow morning at 5 A.M. The next morning 5 people showed up ready to travel.

Mr. Prosper was waiting aboard his remarkably simple boat for the travellers. He welcomed them aboard and they began their long hard journey to the Island of Success. The trip was challenging and the waters were rough day and night for the majority of the journey. As a result, the travellers didn't sleep much. Just a few days into their voyage they were exhausted. On several occasions they were certain that they couldn't continue and asked to turn around. However, each time they managed to encourage one another to keep going. After what seemed like forever they could finally see the island off in the distance. It was the most beautiful thing that they had ever seen. The buildings glimmered brightly and the trees were lush and green. As they reached land they were further astonished and amazed that a place could be so majestic.

Mr. Prosper, who had been silent for most of the trip, called all five travellers to the front of the boat and said, "Congratulations, you've made it to the Island of Success. When I spoke to the crowd, I knew that I was speaking to three types of people: Wannabes, Gottabes, and Gonnabes. The Wannabes said that they wanted to go to the Island of Success so they attended the meeting. However, they gave up on their dream as soon as I started to talk about how difficult the journey would be. The Gottabes not only wanted to go to the Island of Success but they believed that they had to go. They stayed until the end of the meeting but quit just shy of taking the trip. They decided that the journey was too long and too hard so they too gave up. My friends, you are the Gonnabes. Your desire for success was greater than the challenges of the journey. You decided that you would not let anything keep you from your destination. As a result, the Island of Success is yours."

In the story, Mr. Prosper identifies three types of people: Wannabes, Gottabes, and Gonnabes. These three groups all started with success in mind but only the Gonnabes reached their destination. Why? Didn't they all want success? How could people start with the same goal and not get the same results? Most people want to be successful. Or, at least they say that they do. Wannabes say that they want to be successful but they often quit before they start. They talk a good game but they often give up as soon as challenges come. They say that they want success but they only want it if it comes easy. Wannabes are always looking for the shortest and easiest route. They tend to value minimum effort over excellence. If an assignment asks for

3-5 pages the Wannabe is likely going to do only 3 pages, the bare minimum.

The Wannabe jumps from idea to idea rarely achieving success because his/her current "great idea" takes too much work. So, he/she moves on to the next one and repeats this cycle over and over again. Finally, after a few failures the Wannabe may quit entirely because he/she believes that he/she is incapable of success. When in reality the problem is he/she won't stick with any idea or task and work hard enough and long enough to master it.

Gottabes are similar to Wannabes. They too say that they want to be successful but Gottabes go a step further. Gottabes not only say that they want to be successful they believe that they have to be successful. There is a strong motivation behind their pursuit of success, like the desire to better their situation. Unfortunately, having a good motivation doesn't guarantee success. Gottabes may have a little more endurance than Wannabes when challenges come. They may feel that if they quit they are letting themselves or others down. They may endure longer than Wannabes. Eventually, they too quit as soon as the challenge is greater than their motivation.

Meanwhile, Gonnabes have an unstoppable desire for success. No challenge or hardship is great enough to stop their pursuit of it. The Gonnabe will not quit short of his or her success. The Gonnabe is willing to take on any challenge and overcome any obstacle that stands in the way of success. Why? The Gonnabe is not defeated by difficulties that may arise while pursuing his/her success. The Gonnabe understands that hardship is a part of the process. He/she keeps going even in the face of difficulty. No matter how great the difficulty, the Gonnabe sees it as minor in comparison to reaching his/her goals. Gonnabes are obsessed with their success and refuse to acknowledge failure as a possibility. The Gonnabe says, "Either I win or I win. Either I succeed or I succeed. Failure is not an option."

Many people that are not successful don't fall short of success because they're not good enough. It's not because they're not skilled enough. Many people are unsuccessful because their fear of failure prevents them from pursuing their success. Or, it forces them to quit just short of success. Not the Gonnabe. The Gonnabe sets out for success with two options in mind: succeed or succeed. Failure is not an option or possibility. Booker T. Washington once said: "Success is to be measured not so much by the position that one has reached in life as by the obstacles which he has overcome while trying to succeed."

Booker T. Washington was born in Virginia just a few years before the Emancipation Proclamation was signed. He was born a slave and continued to be a slave until after the Civil War ended in 1865. He grew up with his mother, the plantation cook, and his 2 siblings in a windowless cabin. The cabin was barely livable. There were no beds. Washington and his family slept on "filthy rags" on the cabin's bare dirt floor. He had little to no true childhood. He was put to "work" as soon as he was big enough to "clean the yard" or "carry water" to the "workers" in the field.

Washington was not allowed to be educated as it was illegal for slaves to learn to read or write. Washington recalled a time that he carried his owner's daughter's books to school for her. He was deeply inspired by seeing the white boys and girls sitting in the classroom learning. From there a deep desire for education was born. His passion was so great that he said: "...to get into a schoolhouse and study in this way would be about the same as getting into paradise." It would be some time before he would get an education but he continued to dream of being educated.

After the Civil War ended Booker T. Washington and his family were declared free. Soon after he began his quest for an education. He begged his mother for a book even though he couldn't read. She eventually got an old spelling book for him. The book contained the alphabet and basic sounds. With the book he taught himself the alphabet within a few weeks. He had to teach himself because there were no black people near him that could read and teach him. He was too afraid to ask white people for help so he continued on his own for some time.

Eventually a school was opened for freedmen, former slaves, near him. Unfortunately, his stepfather determined that he needed to go work to help support the family. Washington was extremely disappointed but his passion for education never died. He persuaded the local teacher to give him night lessons after work. He persuaded his family to allow him to work early in the morning, go to school, and return to work after school. His school attendance was infrequent and the education that he received was not very good. Washington worked in a coal mine. The work was extremely dangerous. Nevertheless, it was there in that dangerous environment that Washington learned about the opportunity that would change his life. While working he overheard coworkers describing a school for black people in Virginia, called Hampton. At once, Washington determined that he would go to Hampton no matter what it took.

Booker T. Washington set out on a journey to Hampton with very little money and a small bag containing a few pieces of clothing. The distance from his hometown to Hampton was about 500 miles. He walked and begged for rides in wagons and cars. Finally, he managed to get to Richmond, Virginia which was 83 miles from Hampton. By then, he was completely out of money and did not know anyone in the city. He walked the city hungry and without money for food or shelter. Eventually, he slept on the ground under a sidewalk and used his clothes as a pillow. Soon, he found low paying work in Richmond for a short time to pay for food and travel the rest of the way to Hampton. He arrived at Hampton with only $0.50 remaining. His rough appearance after his long journey made the school question admitting him. Nevertheless, he was admitted to Hampton and became a janitor at the school to help pay a portion of his school tuition. Washington excelled at Hampton and was even chosen to speak at his classes' graduation ceremony.

Following his time at Hampton, Washington became an educator in his hometown and eventually at Hampton. He also travelled and gained a reputation for being a great speaker. His excellent speaking ability wowed black and white crowds alike. His ability as an educator was highly regarded as well. Then, the opportunity arose for Mr. Washington to teach black students in Tuskegee, Alabama. However, there was no existing school to teach at. So, Mr. Washington set out on his life work of creating the Tuskegee Institute. The school began in a small "shanty" building with just a few students. Within 7 years the Institute owned over 500 acres of land and had a few hundred students. After 35 years the school owned over 2,000 acres of land, had over 100 staff members, a phenomenal reputation, and over 1500 students. Today, the school started by Washington is known as Tuskegee University and is a national historic landmark. Current students at Tuskegee are reaping the benefits of the foundation that Booker T. Washington laid so many years ago. In 2020, *U.S. News & World Report* ranked Tuskegee 8th out of 80 Historically Black Colleges and Universities. Tuskegee also tied for 25th out of 130+ schools in rankings for best regional schools in the South.

Without a doubt Booker T. Washington was a Gonnabe. He had countless reasons why he couldn't succeed. However, he chose to seek out solutions for the many obstacles that were in front of him. He chose to be successful in spite of the many challenges and adversities that he faced. What will you do with your challenges and adversities? In the next chapter we'll dive deeper into the mindset of the Gonnabe.

## **Let's Think About It**

1. Are you currently a Wannabe, Gottabe, or Gonnabe? How so?

   _____
   _____
   _____
   _____
   _____
   _____

2. What advice would you give to someone who is currently a Wannabe or Gottabe but desires to be a Gonnabe?

   _____
   _____
   _____
   _____
   _____
   _____

3. Why do you think it's so easy for many people to quit short of success? What can you do to safeguard yourself against quitting?

_____

_____

_____

_____

_____

4. If you had the opportunity to ask Booker T. Washington one question, what would you ask him?

_____

_____

_____

_____

_____

5. What is your major takeaway from this chapter? How can you apply it(use it) in your own life?

_____

_____

_____

_____

_____

_____

## *Gonnabe Principle #3*
*"The Gonnabe sets out for success with two options in mind: succeed or succeed."*

# Notes

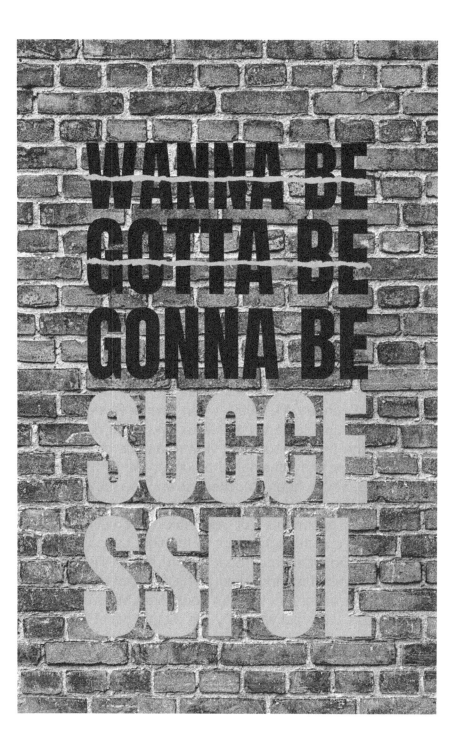

## CHAPTER 4
## GONNA BE SUCCESSFUL

On February 11, 1990, when James Buster Douglas knocked out undefeated "Iron" Mike Tyson, he shocked the world. At the time, Tyson was viewed as one of the fiercest boxers around and considered amongst the all time greats. Tyson had never been knocked down in a boxing match before let alone knocked out. On the contrary, he was known to knock his opponents out very quickly sometimes just a few minutes into the fight. Prior to the fight nobody believed that Buster Douglas could beat Tyson, except Douglas and his mom. Sadly, his mom died just a few weeks before the fight. But her belief that her son could beat Mike Tyson lived on. Douglas was motivated by his mom's belief in him but most importantly he believed that he could beat Mike Tyson. Beating Mike Tyson is just what he did. His victory over the man that once seemed invincible is considered by many as one of the greatest upsets in sports history.

Buster Douglas believed that he could beat Mike Tyson when nearly everyone doubted that he could. It was his belief in himself that made what was seemingly impossible possible. Do you believe in you? Your response to this question is critical. Self belief is greater than your circumstances and greater than other people's opinion of you. If you're gonna be successful you must believe that you will be successful. You must be able to look yourself in the mirror daily and boldly say, " I'm gonna be successful!" If you truly believe that you're gonna be successful you must engrave the thought of your success in your mind with belief. Muhammad Ali once said, "What you're thinking is what you're becoming." One of the most powerful self belief quotes of all time comes from the classic children's book: "The Little Engine That Could". In the book, the Little Engine said, "I think I can, I think I can". Your beliefs are powerful!

Be careful negative beliefs are just as powerful as positive beliefs. If you believe that something is not possible it likely will be impossible for you. You must stand on guard against negative beliefs. The biggest threat to your success is not what's happening around you or what people think about you. Your biggest threat is what's happening in you, in your mind, and what you think about yourself. Our beliefs are affected by what we hear and what we see. Unfortunately, we live in a world that is filled with negativity. As a result, we typically see and hear a lot more negative than we hear and see positive. We're bombarded with negative news from family, friends, social media, and television. There is no shortage of negative news. You may wonder, "How can I think and believe positively when surrounded by so much negativity?" Here are a few ways to protect yourself from negative beliefs:

1. ***Intentionally seek out a consistent source of positive motivation first thing in the morning.*** This can be positive music, spiritual inspiration, reading a

book, watching motivational videos, or engaging in an activity that helps you to think positively such as exercise.

2. **Limit your time around negative people.** You may not be able to completely remove negative people from your life but you can limit the time spent with them.

3. **Limit your time on platforms that give out large amounts of negative news.** Social Media is phenomenal in its ability to help us stay "connected". However, it also makes the spread of news almost instant. Unfortunately, much of this instant news is overwhelmingly negative. Be sure to guard yourself against overdosing on negative news here. Set a time limit on usage each day and stick to it.

Gonnabes are not like most people. While most people go through life with no direction Gonnabes do not. They are very intentional. They operate with a system of beliefs that guide them. Here are 5 beliefs that Gonnabes have that Wannabes and Gottabes do not:

1. **Gonnabes believe that success is not only possible but probable.** Believing that success is possible is easy. In fact, we know that it's possible because we've all seen successful people. However, if you're going to be successful you must believe that success is not only possible but probable, for you. Simply, witnessing someone else's success is not enough. Don't just believe that success can happen. Believe that it will happen for you.

2. **Gonnabes refuse to be average.** Many people unknowingly live with the condition that I like to call "justitis". People with this condition do "just" enough to

get by. At school they do just enough to avoid a failing grade. At work they do just enough to avoid being fired. Not the Gonnabe, the Gonnabe aims for excellence in everything that he/she does. Gonnabes operate in Area 110. Area 110 is reserved for those that give 110% effort in everything that they do.

3. **Gonnabes have a growth mindset.** They believe that where they are today is not where they have to stay forever. Gonnabes know that they have the potential and ability to grow and improve in areas that they currently struggle. They understand that they can get better and better over time. Carol Dweck said: "In a growth mindset, people believe that their most basic abilities can be developed through dedication and hard work—brains and talent are just the starting point. This view creates a love of learning and a resilience that is essential for great accomplishment."

4. **Gonnabes are seekers of true success.** Gonnabes are not solely interested in reaching a reward. Gonnabes are obsessed with maximizing their gift(s) to become the greatest version of themselves. As a result no goal is out of reach. Gonnabes understand that rewards and achievement are byproducts of maximizing one's gift(s).

5. **Gonnabes never quit.** In fact, the word quit doesn't exist in the Gonnabe's vocabulary. Gonnabes value persistence. The Gonnabe understands that success is where the thought of quitting and persistence meet, tussle, and persistence prevails.

The 2016 Cleveland Cavaliers demonstrated each of the 5 beliefs explained above in the 2016 NBA finals. This team did the "impossible". Four games into the NBA Finals the Cavaliers were down 3 games to 1 in their best of 7 game series against the heavily favored Golden State Warriors. In a best of 7 game series the first team to win 4 games wins the series and in this case the NBA championship. The Golden State Warriors only needed to win 1 more game to win the series and the championship. It is important to note that this Golden State Warrior team had the best regular season record in NBA history. During the regular season they won 73 games and only lost 9 times. It is also important to note that no other team has ever come back to win an NBA Finals series after being down 3 games to 1.

The Cavaliers weren't just any team. They were led by "the Kid from Akron", Lebron James. James had returned to play for Cleveland just two years prior, after spending four years playing for the Miami Heat. Against all odds, the Cavaliers won 3 games in a row and won the NBA championship, the franchise's first NBA title. The Cavaliers could have quit in game 5 and accepted that the Warriors were the better team. They could have quit in game 6 and said, "Well, at least we tried". They could have quit in game 7 because they were too tired to fight any longer. Yet, they used none of these excuses. They believed that they could do the impossible and did it. They believed that they were "gonna" be successful. They fought to the very end and were crowned NBA champions as a result.

It was Oprah Winfrey that said: "You don't become what you want, you become what you believe." Oprah Winfrey was born in Mississippi to a teenage mother. Her early years were spent living on a farm with her grandmother. When she was 6 years old she moved to live with her mother in Miluawakee, Wisconsin. While living with her mother, she endured several years of abuse. In her early teens she moved again, this time it was to Nashville, Tennessee to live with her father. Her time with her father had a very positive impact on her life. It was her father who provided her with the stability and discipline that she needed.

At just 19 and a college student at Tennessee State University, Oprah got her start in television as an anchor at a local news station. Following her graduation from college she moved to Baltimore, Maryland and became a reporter and co-anchor for a local news station. Within a year or so Oprah became a co-host of the Baltimore morning show *People are Talking*.

Oprah Winfrey was a natural in front of the camera. In 1984, she found her place in the talk show world. She moved to Chicago, Illinois to take over a struggling talk show. Oprah turned the show around and in 1985 the show was renamed *The Oprah Winfrey Show*. By 1986, the show was the highest rated show in the US and earned several Emmy awards. Around the same time she landed a role in the classic movie, *The Color Purple* and founded her own television production company, Harpo Productions, Inc. Roughly four years later she formed her film production company, Harpo Films. In the year 2000, Oprah launched her magazine, *O Magazine*. By 2011, Oprah had launched a cable network for women, Oxygen Network, debuted a channel on satellite radio, *Oprah and Friends*, and launched the *Oprah Winfrey Network(OWN)*. In addition to her business prowess, Oprah is known for her giving, including a $40 million school for disadvantaged girls in South Africa.

Oprah has been awarded the Jean Hersholt Humanitarian Award from the Academy of Motion Picture Arts and Sciences, the Presidential Medal of Freedom, and the Cecil B. DeMille Award (a Golden Globe for lifetime achievement). She also holds honorary doctorate degrees from Princeton, Howard University, Duke University, and Harvard University. Today, her net worth is nearly $3 billion.

As of the year 2020, she is the tenth richest self made woman in the U.S.

Oprah Winfrey has achieved more than most of us can even imagine. Her road was not easy. In fact, it was tough and filled with obstacles and challenges. In spite of it all Oprah believed in Oprah. She believed that she was "gonna" be successful. Her unshakable belief is the foundation of her massive success. She is proof that nothing is impossible if you just believe and act on that belief.

## Let's Think About It

1. What are some ways that you can personally reduce the negative influences in your life?

   _____

   _____

   _____

   _____

   _____

   _____

2. List 3 sources of positive influences that you can rely on consistently.

   _____

   _____

   _____

   _____

   _____

   _____

3. Which of the 5 Gonnabe beliefs do you need to work on developing the most?

_____

_____

_____

_____

_____

4. If you had the opportunity to ask Oprah Winfrey one question, what would you ask her?

_____

_____

_____

_____

_____

5. What is your major takeaway from this chapter? How can you apply it(use it) in your own life?

_____

_____

_____

_____

_____

_____

### ***Gonnabe Principle # 4***
*"Nothing is impossible for you if you just believe that it is possible. "*

## Notes

# Gifted

# CHAPTER 5
## GIFTED

In 2019, experts estimated that Americans would spend over $1 trillion on Christmas gifts. Yes, you read it correctly, Americans were expected to spend over $1,000,000,000,000 on Christmas gifts. Yet, many of the gifts would likely go unappreciated, underused, or even unused by those that received them. Think about the gifts that you received from your most recent Christmas. How many gifts did you continue to use 30 days after Christmas? How many did continue to use 6 months after Christmas? How many are you still using, now? So much time, effort, and thought is spent on gifts that will be meaningless shortly after they are purchased. I'd like to suggest that the greatest gifts are not found not under a Christmas tree but within us. Yet, like Christmas gifts, many of us allow our gifts to go unappreciated, underused, or even unused.

Long ago, back when dinosaurs roamed the earth I was an elementary school student. At my school there was a class known as Gifted and Talented. On certain days the Gifted and Talented teacher would go around to each class and pick up her Gifted and Talented students. Then, they'd go off to a separate classroom. I hated it when she came. I hated it because each time that the Gifted and Talented group left I was reminded that I wasn't part of the group. I felt excluded and hurt. I remember asking myself, "Why can't I go?" I made pretty good grades. Yet, I didn't make the cut. If we're honest with ourselves most of us have felt rejected or excluded at some point. You may be even feeling rejected in some area of your life now. If so, please understand that rejection or exclusion does not invalidate you or make you less. There is more than one type of smart. There is more than one type of gifted. Every person possesses a unique gift. Your gift is a natural ability or capacity that you possess. It comes easy to you but difficult for others. It is the thing that you were "born to do". Your gift is your superpower!

Several years later while in 9th grade I had the unfortunate experience of taking a public speaking class. I refer to this experience as unfortunate because speaking in front of people was one of my biggest fears at the time. I am naturally an introvert and was convinced that I would die on the spot if I ever had to. When the day of my speech finally came I was terrified. I was panicking internally but I was too "cool" to let the class see me sweat. I was certain that I'd either faint or go mute when I stood to speak. To my surprise neither happened. My heart was racing like Usain Bolt but I somehow made it through the speech. I wish that I could share with you what I spoke about and how profound it was but I can't. In fact, I don't remember much about the class. What I do recall is what my teacher said to me after my first speech. She said, "You're going to be a public speaker, one day." I thought, "Lady, that has to be one of the dumbest things that I've ever heard in my life. Do you not realize that

I almost died up there?" I was afraid and unsure of myself but somehow I managed to complete my speech, alive.

As terrified as I was I'm grateful for my experience in that high school speech class because it helped me face my fear and find my gift. I'm still somewhat of an introvert and I still get "butterflies" in my stomach everytime that I speak. Nevertheless, I have the honor and privilege of speaking to and empowering thousands of students. I am a speaker today partly because my speech teacher saw something in me that I couldn't see in myself. She saw my gift and planted a seed of possibility in my mind. That seed gave me a small glimpse of what I was capable of. I had a gift and didn't even know it. The gift that you need to be successful is already in you. It's there waiting to be discovered and revealed to the world.

My immediate reaction was to dismiss my teacher's "prophesy" that I would one day be a public speaker. I was so uncomfortable speaking in front of others that I convinced myself that she had to be wrong. Following that class I didn't speak in front of a group again until my first year of college. To my surprise my public speaking professor's feedback sounded much like the feedback that I received from that "crazy" speech teacher in 9th grade. Other people's perspective is invaluable because of the unique perspective from which they view your gift. When you look at you it's easy to only see limitations, shortcomings, fears, and flaws. On the contrary, other people have a more objective view of you. In other words, their perspective is not clouded or distorted by your flaws. For this reason it is wise to seek out feedback from qualified individuals.

In my case, it was easy getting feedback from my teacher and professors because feedback was expected in the classroom setting. However, you may not be using your gift in a classroom setting that allows you to receive immediate feedback. You may need to be a little more intentional. To do so make a list of 3 to 5 trustworthy individuals that know you really well. Your list can include your parents, teachers, counselors, coaches, and so on. Once you've created your list, ask each individual to identify 3 things that you do better than most people or what you're really gifted in. Once you've gathered the responses compare the lists. Identify the areas that the lists have in common. Now that you have ideas about what your gift might be, you need to test them. Seek out opportunities to discover and confirm your gift. Find volunteer roles at school, church, in your community, and other venues that will allow you to discover your gift. Keep seeking until your gift/super power becomes evident. Remember, your gift is something that you do that comes easy to you but is difficult for others.

Having a gift is not enough. Success begins with the maximization of your gift. In order to maximize your gift you have to use it. Jose was determined to become a professional bodybuilder. He'd always heard that he had the perfect body type for it. Finally, he decided that he'd try to become a bodybuilder. For the next 6 months he spent 2 hours at the gym 7 days per week. At the end of this 6 month period he was devastated that his body didn't change. His body looked exactly as it had 6 months prior. He was frustrated. So, he hired a personal trainer and told her about his struggles from the previous 6 months. He told her how he'd been going to the gym for 6 months and never missed a day. She was shocked that he wasn't getting results that he desired. Then, she probed further. Within a matter of minutes she found his problem. Even though he had been going to the gym everyday for 6 months he wasn't working out. He would go to the gym everyday and watch YouTube videos of bodybuilders for 2 hours. Many people are just like this "aspiring" bodybuilder. They say that they want to be successful but they refuse to commit. Like Jose they sit around hoping to miraculously get results without putting in the work. If you want to maximize your gift and realize your full potential you must commit to growing your gift through exercise/practice.

What is stopping you from pursuing and maximizing your gift? Are you afraid of what people will say or think of you? Many people are more concerned with what people think about them than they are about being successful. When you begin to walk in your gift there will be haters. There will be people that don't like you. There will be people that don't think you're good enough. So what! Grammy Award winning Rapper Lecrae said it best, "If you live for their acceptance you'll die from their rejection." Don't spend energy and effort trying to impress people who are set on hating you. Madam C.J. Walker said, "Now I realize that in the so-called higher walks of life, many were prone to look down upon hairdressers as they called us; they didn't have a very high opinion of our calling, so I had to go down and dignify this work, so much so that many of the best women of our race are now engaged in this line of business, and many of them are now in my employ."

Madam C.J. Walker identified her gift and maximized it. As a result she became extremely successful. She accumulated a massive fortune but more importantly she was able to be a blessing to others. I can't guarantee you Madam Walker's impact or wealth. However, I can assure you that if you pursue your gift and maximize it success awaits you.

Madam C.J. Walker was born into poverty in Louisiana shortly after the end of slavery. She worked washing clothes and cleaning the homes of wealthy families. While working for the wealthy she took notice of how they cared for their appearance. She wanted to help black women also take pride in their appearance. So, she began developing a hair care system that would further enhance the natural beauty of black women. When she wasn't working at her job as a cleaning lady she was working at her passion, testing hair care formulas. Eventually, she developed the "Walker Comb" and a hair care treatment system that would straighten black hair and make dull dry hair look soft and natural. Next, she developed a full line of products and opened her own manufacturing facility. She initially sold her products door to door. Madam C.J. Walker's business exploded. Before her death she had hired 2,000+ women who served as sales reps, which she called Walker Agents. Her business was a huge success and she became America's first black female millionaire.

Madam C.J. Walker was truly remarkable. She shocked the world with her success. She even caught the attention of the great Booker T. Washington. In 1912, Madam C.J. Walker famously interrupted Booker T. Washington's National Negro Business League Convention. After being denied the opportunity to speak at the convention because she was a woman, she stood up on the last day of the convention and boldly said to Mr. Washington, "Surely you are not going to shut the door in my face, I have been trying to tell you what I am doing. I am a woman who came from the cotton fields of the South. I was promoted from there to the washtub. Then I was promoted to the cook kitchen. And from there I promoted myself into the business of manufacturing hair goods and preparations. I know how to grow hair as well as I know how to grow cotton. I have built my own factory on my own ground." The following year Madam Walker was invited to present at the conference. She was also well known for using a portion of her fortune for charity. She notably donated to help build the first black YMCA in Indianapolis, Indiana. She also helped restore the home of the great Frederick Douglas and financially supported the NAACP's anti lynching program.

Madam C.J. Walker used her gift to help black women embrace and further enhance their beauty. Her business changed the face of black women in business and women in business in general. Her gift and passion for serving women allowed her to impact thousands upon thousands of women through providing employment and products that catered to the needs of black women. Madam Walker impacted the world and it started with her commitment to maximizing her gift. I challenge you to find your gift, begin the process of maximizing it, and then go impact the world. King Solomon said, "Your gift will make room for you and sit you before the great." Hard work may help you earn a living but your gift will help you live your dreams.

# Let's Think About It

1. Has there ever been a time when you didn't feel gifted enough? Please explain.

   _____

   _____

   _____

   _____

   _____

   _____

2. What is your gift(s)? Note: Your gift comes natural to you and you do it better than most with little to no effort.

   _____

   _____

   _____

   _____

   _____

   _____

3. List 3 people that know you well that can help you identify your gift(s)?

_____

_____

_____

_____

_____

4. If you had the opportunity to ask Madam C.J. Walker one question, what would you ask her?

_____

_____

_____

_____

_____

5. What is your major takeaway from this chapter? How can you apply it (use it) in your own life?

_____

_____

_____

_____

_____

_____

**Gonnabe Principle # 5**
*"There is more than one type of smart. There is more than one type of gifted. "*

## Notes

# CHAPTER 6
# DEFINITE DESTINATION

"I have a dream." Dr. Martin Luther King Jr. spoke these powerful words in his famous "I Have a Dream" speech in 1963. His speech shook the nation to its core regarding the fight for equality. What started in his mind has since captured the hearts and minds of millions. Mankind's ability to dream is a quality that puts him far and above the animals. As powerful as it may be, even the mighty lion in all of his majesty can only be a lion. The lion has no ability to change its circumstances, unless of course it's name is Simba. Young man or young lady you have the unique ability to dream and become what you dreamed about.

If you're going to be successful you must dream big. You must be able to see what you want to become before you become it. You must be able to see who you want to become before you can become that person. Dr. King dreamed his dream and saw what he wanted the world to look like long before it started to look that way. Our nation is far from living out Dr. King's dream. Yet, it has made considerable progress largely because he dared to dream.

I dare you to dream. A dream is an attainable vision for your future. However, while dreaming you have to be able to distinguish between dream and fantasy. A fantasy is a vision that is not attainable in the real world. Let me give you an example. Several years ago two of my coworkers got into an argument. One began to criticize the other saying that he wasn't working hard enough. He replied, "I don't want to work here, anyway. I wanted to be a baseball player." At the time, this gentleman was approaching 40 years old and not nearly physically fit enough to be a professional baseball player. In fact, I'm not sure that he'd ever played competitive baseball. Nevertheless, he was still holding on to this childhood fantasy of playing professional baseball. I'm not sharing this story to make fun of my former coworker. I share this story to highlight the sad reality that far too many people are chasing unattainable fantasies instead of pursuing their dreams. Truth is it's a lot easier to fantasize than it is to pursue hard after your dreams. A fantasy requires no action. On the other hand, taking action is the first step to realizing your dream.

Dr. King's dream led him to take action and because he knew what he wanted he was able to rally people around his dream. He spoke out boldly against injustice and stood for those that couldn't stand up for themselves. The dream that began in his mind spurred him into action. His action thrusted him to the forefront of the civil rights movement. So much so that it's hard to think of the civil rights movement without Dr. King coming to mind. Your dream should lead you to take action. The first necessary action is to transition your dream into a goal.

Goals help us to clearly define what we want to accomplish. In other words, goals help us to create a definite destination or target. Lack of a definite destination leads to wandering. One of things that I most hate about driving is when I find myself behind a wanderer, someone who has no idea where they're going. They go, brake, and stop repeatedly. Every several hundred feet or so they act as if they're going to turn but don't. They frequently use false turn signals as they aimlessly search for their destination. Meanwhile, I'm delayed in getting to my destination until I'm able to maneuver around them. Don't be a wanderer. Success requires having a definite destination in mind. Failure to have a definite destination will delay you in getting to where you want to go, or may even prevent you from getting there at all.

Imagine one day coming home to find a letter addressed to you. You open the letter and discover that you have been gifted with $1,000,000. The letter lists an address that is nearly 1,500 miles away from your home. To receive the $1,000,000 gift you must travel to the address listed on the letter. $1,000,000 is waiting for you. It's been assigned to you. You just need to go and get it. You wouldn't dare walk out of the door without directions or a strategy to get to your destination. Nor would you let anything distract you on your journey. Why? Because there is too much at stake to just wander. Likewise, you shouldn't dare attempt to embark on your journey to success without a definite destination and plan to reach it. Having a definite destination will enable you to see your end goal and create a plan to reach it. If you want to reach and achieve the goals that you've set for yourself you have to have a crystal clear picture of what your goals are. Pursuing success without a definite destination is like attempting to put a complicated 10,000 piece puzzle together without a picture of the finished puzzle. It's nearly impossible.

You must clearly identify your definite destination or goals. When setting goals be specific and state exactly what you want to accomplish. Vague goals don't get accomplished. It is also extremely important to note the timeframe in which you intend to accomplish the goal. There are short range, mid range, and long range goals. Short range goals are goals that you set with the expectation of accomplishing them in a year or less. Mid range goals are goals that you would like to accomplish within 1 to 5 years. Long range goals are goals that will take 5 to 10 years to accomplish. Meet Tasha. Tasha is a high school sophomore at GBS Academy. Tasha's short range goal is to finish the Fall semester with an A in her Algebra class. Her mid range goal is to get accepted into the prestigious Howard University. Tasha's long range goal is to found and operate a non profit organization that trains underprivileged youth in entrepreneurship. Notice that all of Tasha's goals are very specific. She doesn't just say that she wants to make a "good grade" in Algebra. No. She names her grade. She doesn't settle for saying that she just wants to go to college. Instead, she names her college of choice. Lastly, she doesn't just say that she wants to work with kids someday. No. She identifies an organization that she will create to work with children. To be effective your goals must be clear and specific.

Once you've identified your goals, you must pursue them fiercely and make them your primary focus. Everything unrelated to your goals should be secondary. When pursuing your goals you may have to make some hard decisions. For instance if you set a goal to fund your college education with scholarships, free money awarded to selected students to pay for college, your primary focus should be applying for scholarships. You should set aside designated time on the weekend and/or outside of school hours to research and apply for scholarships. Millions of dollars of scholarship money goes unawarded each year because people simply don't apply. Many people desire scholarship money but very few prioritize applying. If you desire to receive scholarship money you have to commit to the process, focus on your goal, and remove distractions that might prevent you from reaching your goal. Then, set boundaries for yourself to ensure that you're fully focused on your goal. To fully focus you may have to disconnect yourself from social media and other distractions that may demand your attention. Be sure to set designated times for scholarship applications. During these times make it clear to your family and friends that you are unavailable. Your friends may initially be disappointed with your lack of availability due to your new focus. However, if they are true friends they will applaud and support your effort to better yourself.

Unfortunately, focusing on your goals is easier said than done. There will be many distractions along the way. Things that were not previously distractions may become distractions as you attempt to focus on your goal. If you find yourself struggling to consistently focus, create a routine. Creating a routine can be really helpful in helping you become more disciplined, organized, and consistent. A routine is a regularly scheduled set of activities. An example of a routine would be working on scholarship applications every Saturday from 2 pm until 4 pm. If you struggle initially to maintain focus the entire it is OK. Stay consistent with your routine and you'll notice that your ability to focus will increase.

Many people fail to accomplish their goals because they get discouraged that they're not seeing immediate results and quit. A way to avoid this is to highlight and celebrate small wins. Small wins occur when you complete the small steps and tasks necessary to help you reach your goal. An example of a small win would be beginning your scholarship application session at the scheduled time for an entire week. Like in sports lots of small wins lead to championships. On the other hand, hold yourself accountable when you're not making progress towards achieving your goal. Be sure to designate what your rewards and consequences will be in advance and put them in writing. Make sure that your accountability is clear and realistic.

### **Examples of Rewards and Consequences:**

**Reward**: If I spend at least an hour each day this week applying for scholarships, I will treat myself to a special meal.

**Consequence**: If I fail to apply for 10 scholarships this week, I will not have dessert this week.

     Goal setting is not optional, it is absolutely necessary. You will never be who you want to be until you can see who you want to be. Then, set goals to become that person. I understand that this may be hard to comprehend because many of us have been trained to only believe what we can see. Dr. Tony Evans often says, "If all you see is what you see you have not seen all there is to be seen." You don't have to see your dream before you can believe it, but you do have to believe it before you'll ever see it. Dream, set goals, and take action.

     Arthur G. Gaston, also known as A.G. Gaston was a man with goals. His maternal grandparents, both former slaves, raised him in rural Alabama during his early years. He later moved to live with his mother in the city of Birmingham, Alabama. His mother had relocated years earlier in search of more opportunity. Gaston attended school at the famous Tuggle Institute. It was here that he met and was deeply influenced by Booker T. Washington, who would often visit and speak to the school's students.

Though he did not finish school Gaston was positively impacted by his time at the Tuggle Institute.

Gaston worked many jobs and developed a very strong work ethic early on. He had a great reputation with all of his employers. When he turned 21, he enlisted in the military and served in an all black regiment in World War I. Following his military service, Gaston returned to society to find very limited employment opportunities. So, he secured work in one of the few places available to him at the time, the iron and coal mines. The pay was miserable and the working conditions were equally bad. For most of the workers the coal and iron mines is where they would work for the rest of their lives but not A.G. Gaston. He had dreams and goals to achieve.

Opportunity first presented itself during lunch time. Gaston's mom would prepare him home cooked meals for lunch. Many of the other men didn't have the luxury of having home cooked meals prepared for their lunch. So, Gaston began to serve his fellow mine workers, literally. His mom began preparing extra lunches and he would sell them to his coworkers. He also picked up other "hustles" such as selling popcorn and peanuts. Eventually, these small business ventures allowed him to save a good deal of money. Instead of wasting his money partying like many of his coworkers, Gaston figured out a way to use his savings to make more money. He began lending money to his coworkers. His offer was extremely attractive because the banks refused to lend to them. So, a loan from Gaston was often the only option available to them. These hustles grew his understanding of business and prepared him for what the future would hold.

Many would have been content to continue with these small business ventures within the mines. However, A.G. Gaston was far from content. He had much bigger goals in mind. He spent a lot of time thinking of other business ideas. Then, he began looking at his community and assessing what the needs of the community were. Gaston recalled that each payday individuals would solicit donations from Gaston and other mine workers. These individuals were allegedly raising money to cover funeral expenses for recently deceased loved ones. At the time, poor families did not have the money to cover the funeral and burial expenses for loved ones. So, they would ask for assistance from the community. Unfortunately, many scammers took advantage of this practice and tricked sympathetic donors out of their hard earned money. Gaston saw a problem and created a solution to solve it.

In 1923, A.G. Gaston created the Booker T. Washington Burial Society, which would later become the Booker T. Washington Insurance Company. The company assisted poor black families by providing policies that would help cover final expenses for their deceased loved ones. The initial insurance policies were sold door to door. The company eventually grew into a massive operation and would be one of Gaston's most successful businesses. A.G. Gaston went on to do the "impossible" by becoming a successful black businessman and millionaire, in the heart of the "Jim Crow South". His success was extremely uncommon at the time. It demonstrates that the impossible is possible when you know what you want.

Gaston used his great wealth to help others. He was very influential in the Civil Rights Movement. In fact, he personally bailed Dr. Martin Luther King Jr. out of jail during his famous stay in which he wrote " Letter from Birmingham Jail". Later in life Gaston famously sold the Booker T. Washington Insurance company to his employees for just $3.5 million even though the company was worth over $30 million. Some people thought that he was crazy for selling the company for so little. He wasn't crazy at all. He was grateful for employees for their role in helping him build the business. The sale was a very generous display of his gratitude.

A.G. Gaston had a definite destination in mind and passionately pursued it. He accumulated a lot of wealth but wealth was not his primary goal. His goal was to use his wealth to help others. He said: "Money's no good unless it contributes something to the community, unless it builds a bridge to a better life. Any man can make money, but it takes a special kind of man to use it responsibly." The day before he turned 100 years old, Black Enterprise Magazine named him the Entrepreneur of the Century. He lived to be 103 years old and left a legacy that will never be forgotten.

# Let's Think About It

1. Take a few moments and visualize where you see yourself in five years. What do you see?

   _____

   _____

   _____

   _____

   _____

   _____

2. Do you have written goals for yourself? Why or why not?

   _____

   _____

   _____

   _____

   _____

   _____

3. What is/are your goal/goals for this school year?

_____

_____

_____

_____

_____

_____

4. If you had the opportunity to ask A.G. Gaston one question, what would you ask him?

_____

_____

_____

_____

_____

_____

5. What is your major takeaway from this chapter? How can you apply it(use it) in your own life?

_____

_____

_____

_____

_____

### <u>Gonnabe Principle # 6</u>
" You don't have to see your dream before you can believe it but you do have to believe it before you'll ever see it. "

## Notes

# CHAPTER 7
# YOUR SUCCESS IS IN YOUR PLAN

Growing up, I remember playing Nintendo and later Sega Genesis for hours at a time. I also remember quitting games out of frustration with my inability to get past a certain level or stage of the game. Some sessions would end with me throwing a game controller and angrily storming out of my room. I enjoyed playing the games but honestly I was never very good. That was until I discovered the Game Genie. The Game Genie contained cheat codes. It allowed players to bypass levels, gain extra lives, and more. It transformed average players into great players. I'd like to suggest that having a plan is like having a Game Genie. An effective plan is the success cheat code. A great plan can transport an individual from average to great.

In the previous chapter we talked about determining a definite destination or setting goals. Having goals are great but simply having goals is not enough. Simply having goals won't help you accomplish them. Just like the desire to travel to an unknown destination is insufficient by itself. The desire must be partnered with directions to reach the desired location. A plan is like a map or GPS system that helps you navigate the path to accomplishing your goals.

There was a young man who was nearing the end of his high school career. Graduation was only 30 days away. One Saturday morning, his grandfather called and said, "I'm so proud of you. It has been my pleasure to watch you grow into the phenomenal young man that you're becoming. Let's have lunch next Saturday." The young man agreed. He loved spending time with his grandfather. In addition to picking the best restaurants in town he was extremely wise. The young man dreamed of the day that he'd have half of his grandfather's wisdom. His grandfather picked him up the following Saturday for lunch. During lunch the young man said, "Grandpa, you've been so successful all of these years and even trained your kids, my dad and Aunt GiGi, to do the same. I want to be just like you. What's the secret?" His grandfather chuckled and replied, " Son, there's no secret. I made up my mind many years ago that I was gonna be successful. I set goals, created a plan to achieve my goals, and decided that I would not let anything stop me."

The pair finished their meal and headed home. The young man was silent for most of the ride home as he pondered his grandfather's words. Finally, he spoke and said, "Grandpa, I have a really cool idea that I want to tell you about." Before he could share his idea his grandfather stopped him and said, "I'll pick you up next Saturday at 6:30am for breakfast. Be sure to write out your idea and your plan to bring it to life." Even though he hated waking up early the young man was excited to share his idea with his grandfather. His grandfather picked him the following Saturday at 6:30am sharp. Then, they headed to the Natural

Foods Store for breakfast. After they finished their food the young man was eager to share his idea with his grandfather. Before he could share his grandfather asked, "Did you write out your idea and your plan to accomplish it?" The young man replied, " No. I didn't write it down but I promise you that it's really good." His grandfather responded, "I'm not interested." The young man was devastated and wondered how his grandfather had lost interest so quickly.

The ride home was filled with tension. Anger and disappointment was visible on the young man's face. As they pulled into his driveway his grandfather asked, " Why are you angry?" The young man said, "Grandpa, you told me that you wanted to hear my idea but you shut me down when I tried to tell you about it". His grandfather replied, "Son, I asked you to write out your idea and your plan to accomplish it. I did not tell you this to waste your time. I told you to write your idea out because your success is in your plan. When you look at me you see success. When I look at me I see the plan that I created over 40 years ago coming to life. Before your dad was born I decided that I was going to change my family for the better by building a successful business. When I started all I had were my goals and my plan. Today, our family business owns over 200 properties and provides high quality affordable housing for people that need it most. Most people are walking around with lots of great ideas in their mind. Unfortunately, most never transfer those ideas into a plan. As a result, they never see their dreams come true. Your success is in your plan, young man. Never forget that."

Success doesn't just happen to you. Your success is in your plan. There are many people that are extremely gifted. These people seem to be destined for success but without a plan the likelihood of success is slim to none for even the best of these. Planning is not just important it is absolutely necessary for success. Here are 3 reasons why:

1. A plan helps you see the end before you begin. In the previous chapter, we talked about having clear and precise goals in mind. A plan allows you to pinpoint what it is that you want to accomplish before you begin the process. Most people are not successful because they don't know where they want to end up. As a result, they end up wherever life takes them.

2. A plan helps you develop a clear path to accomplishing your goals. Success doesn't happen all at once. It comes in steps. Each step along the way is critical to reaching your goals. Just as each turn is critical to arriving at your desired destination when driving.

3. A plan helps you to monitor your progress. Many people quit just short of success because they don't realize how close they are to success. Planning will allow you to see how close or how far you are away from your goals.

A wise person once said, "If you fail to plan you plan to fail". If you don't plan you'll find yourself in a situation that you don't want to be in for longer than you want to be there. Planning requires you to take a glimpse into the future and see the future you, the successful you. This may be difficult because it's hard to imagine a you that doesn't exist yet. It may be difficult to imagine yourself accomplishing goals that now seem impossible. Don't be discouraged. Trust the process and know that as you take the necessary steps towards your goals your capacity to achieve those goals will grow as you grow. Research your favorite professional. I guarantee that they did not begin where they are now. The best doctors, educators, lawyers, engineers, corporate executives, and entrepreneurs were once your age. They had dreams that they transformed into goals. Then, they created a plan to accomplish those goals. Fashion Mogul

Daymond John knows the importance of a plan. It is so critical to his success that he says, "Five days a week, I read my goals before I go to sleep and when I wake up."

Today, many know Daymond John as a refined businessman and investor on the hit TV Series, Shark Tank. I first heard about Daymond when I was in high school. He was a young rising entrepreneur with a fast growing clothing brand, FUBU. Daymond was one of the first entrepreneurs that inspired me to begin thinking about entrepreneurship. It was very easy for me to relate to him and the brand that he was building. His brand spoke a language that I understood, hip hop. It was raw and fresh just like hip hop and I felt connected to it instantly.

From the time he was a kid Daymond always had an entrepreneurial spirit. From shoveling snow in his neighborhood of Hollis Queens in New York City to offering a pre-Uber ride share service he was figuring out ways to earn money. Daymond was raised in a single parent household by his mother. He was dyslexic and struggled in school with reading and writing. Nevertheless, Daymond was a Gonnabe, he was determined to be successful. While working full time as a waiter at Red Lobster Daymond developed an idea for a clothing brand. His mother taught him to sew and he began sewing hats by hand in his mother's home.

The hats that Daymond sewed began to sell really well and FUBU was born. Daymond grew his brand and added T-Shirts. The brand really took off when Daymond executed a plan to get up and coming hip-hop artists to wear his brand in their music videos. An artist would wear the shirt, return the shirt to Daymond, he would have it cleaned, and pass it on to the next artist. FUBU was this really small scrappy company operating out of Daymond's mom's house. However, FUBU seemed like a big deal from the outside looking in. The brand gained a lot of attention thanks to the influence of these hip hop artists, including all time great LL COOL J. Early on Daymond didn't have the money to get his brand in front of customers through paid advertising. So, he got creative and his innovative plan helped him reach his audience for little to no cost.

FUBU was one of the premiere streetwear brands in the country in the late 1990's and early 2000's. Some would say that Daymond and his friends simply got lucky. This is true if you define luck as a plan meeting great opportunity. That's exactly what happened with Daymond and FUBU. FUBU has sold $6 billion of merchandise in 5,000 stores, according to FUBU.com. Daymond is still going strong, building a massive business portfolio and executing his plans.

You may not have a desire to build a brand or start a business. Nevertheless, we can all learn a very important and profound lesson from Daymond's success story. Planning makes all the difference. It was Daymond's effective planning that allowed FUBU to become a household name. If you desire to be successful you must commit to planning. As proven by Daymond's story your success is truly in your plan. An effective plan will help you think through and navigate obstacles and challenges. Ultimately, your plan will serve as your guide to achieving your goals.

## Let's Think About It

1. Why is setting goals alone not enough to become successful?

_____

_____

_____

_____

_____

_____

2. How is it that someone can be extremely gifted and unsuccessful at the same time?

_____

_____

_____

_____

_____

_____

3. Do you have a written plan for your success? If so, what/who inspired you to write it? If not, what's keeping you from writing it?

_____

_____

_____

_____

_____

_____


4. If you had the opportunity to ask Daymond John one question, what would you ask him?

_____

_____

_____

_____

_____

_____

5. What is your major takeaway from this chapter? How can you apply it(use it) in your own life?

_____

_____

_____

_____

_____

_____

## Gonnabe Principle # 7
*"Success doesn't just happen to you. Your success is in your plan."*

# Notes

# Gonna Be Successful Planner

In chapter 7, Your Success is in Your Plan, we discussed how important your plan is to your success. On the following pages you'll have the opportunity to create your own plan. Your plan can focus on school, college preparation, or an area of your choice. Your plan will consist of the following components:

1. **Vision Statement:** Your vision statement should be two to three sentences long. Ultimately, your vision statement is a snapshot of what you want for your life and your future.

   *Example*: *To become the best student that I can be. And to bring about positive change in my community.*

2. **Goals**: Your goals are your desired results for your future. Goals should always be clear and precise and never vague.

   *Example*: *My goal is to earn an A+ in my history class.*

3. **Action Steps:** Action steps are the steps and tasks required to ensure that your goals become reality.

   *Example*: *In order to accomplish my goal of earning an A+ in history class I must study 6+ hours outside of class time each week.*

4. **Strengths and Weaknesses:** Strengths and Weaknesses are your abilities and inabilities to perform in certain areas. Most of us can easily point out our strengths but struggle to identify our weaknesses. It is important that we be able to identify both. Knowing your strengths will help you focus on what you're good at and emphasize those areas. On the other hand, knowing your weaknesses is important too. Understanding your weaknesses will help you identify the areas that you struggle in and which areas you will need the most assistance.

   *Example of Strengths*: *My strengths are my communication skills, technical skills, and creativity.*

*Examples of Weaknesses:* My weaknesses are my organization skills, time management, and procrastination.

5. **Success Team:** Your success team is perhaps one of the most important pieces of your plan. Your success team is made up of people that you have selected to hold you accountable for working your plan. Your success team should be made up of two groups of people: coaches and teammates.

   *Coach(es):* One or more people who will serve as an authority figure. Coaches are typically older and/or more experienced. Coaches can be teachers, counselors, mentors, pastors, etc.

   *Teammates:* Teammates are peers that have a similar focus. Be careful in selecting teammates because the wrong teammates can be detrimental to your success. Your teammates should be people that are as motivated or more motivated than you.

# Gonna Be Successful Planner

**Vision Statement:**

_____

_____

_____

*Short Range Goal (1 year):*

_____

_____

_____

**Mid Range Goal (1 to 5 years):**

_____

_____

_____

**Long Range Goal (5 to 10 years):**

_____

_____

_____

_____

*Action Steps:*

_____

_____

_____

_____

_____

## Success Team

*Coaches:*

_____

_____

_____


*Teammates:*

_____

_____

_____

# Gonna Be Successful 30-Day Challenge

OK. You've taken in lots of information and you've even had a chance to create your success plan. Now, I'd like to challenge you to go a step further. In this challenge you will need to be very intentional in working towards achieving one of your goals for the next 30 days. Each day you will need to write out your goal and the action steps that you must take to reach your goal. At the end of each day you will grade yourself on whether or not you successfully completed that day's action steps. 30 days may seem intimidating initially but it's really not as bad it seems. Investing in this challenge will be well worth your time. It will help you further develop the consistency that you need to be successful.

Recite your goal and your action steps aloud twice each day, once in the morning and once before you go to sleep. Repeating your goal and action steps each day will help you train your mind to believe that your goal is attainable. Some days you may have only 1 action step and 4 on other days. There is no right or wrong answer for the number of action steps for each day. However, you should be taking some type of action step towards your goal daily. Get started! Execution is greater than perfection. Don't worry about getting everything just right. Remember, small wins count. Do something everyday! Each week share your progress with your success team. Please see the example on the next page.

**Example:**

**_Day 27_**

**Goal:** _I will make an A in my history class this semester._

**Action Step**: _Study for 30 minutes after dinner._

**Completed(Yes or No):** Yes

**Action Step**: _Attend study group after school._

**Complete(Yes or No)**: No

**Action Step**: _Write introduction for my research paper._

**Complete(Yes No)**: Yes

## Day 1

**Goal:** _____

**Action Step:** _____

**Completed(Yes or No):** _____


**Action Step:** _____

**Complete(Yes or No):** _____


**Action Step:** _____

**Completed(Yes or No):** _____


## Day 2

**Goal:** _____

**Action Step:** _____

**Completed(Yes or No):** _____


**Action Step:** _____

**Complete(Yes or No):** _____


**Action Step:** _____

**Completed(Yes or No):** _____

## Day 3

Goal: _____

Action Step: _____

Completed(Yes or No): _____

Action Step: _____

Complete(Yes or No): _____

Action Step: _____

Completed(Yes or No): _____

## Day 4

Goal: _____

Action Step: _____

Completed(Yes or No): _____

Action Step: _____

Complete(Yes or No): _____

Action Step: _____

Completed(Yes or No): _____

## Day 5

**Goal:** _____

**Action Step:** _____

**Completed(Yes or No):** _____

**Action Step:** _____

**Complete(Yes or No):** _____

**Action Step:** _____

**Completed(Yes or No):** _____

## Day 6

**Goal:** _____

**Action Step:** _____

**Completed(Yes or No):** _____

**Action Step:** _____

**Complete(Yes or No):** _____

**Action Step:** _____

**Completed(Yes or No):** _____

## Day 7

Goal: _____

Action Step: _____

Completed(Yes or No): _____


Action Step: _____

Complete(Yes or No): _____


Action Step: _____

Completed(Yes or No): _____

## Day 8

Goal: _____

Action Step: _____

Completed(Yes or No): _____


Action Step: _____

Complete(Yes or No): _____


Action Step: _____

Completed(Yes or No): _____

**Day 9**

Goal: _____

Action Step: _____

Completed(Yes or No): _____

Action Step: _____

Complete(Yes or No): _____

Action Step: _____

Completed(Yes or No): _____

**Day 10**

Goal: _____

Action Step: _____

Completed(Yes or No): _____

Action Step: _____

Complete(Yes or No): _____

Action Step: _____

Completed(Yes or No): _____

**Day 11**

Goal: _____

Action Step: _____

Completed(Yes or No): _____

Action Step: _____

Complete(Yes or No): _____

Action Step: _____

Completed(Yes or No): _____

**Day 12**

Goal: _____

Action Step: _____

Completed(Yes or No): _____

Action Step: _____

Complete(Yes or No): _____

Action Step: _____

Completed(Yes or No): _____

**Day 13**

Goal: _____

Action Step: _____

Completed(Yes or No): _____

Action Step: _____

Complete(Yes or No): _____

Action Step: _____

Completed(Yes or No): _____

**Day 14**

Goal: _____

Action Step: _____

Completed(Yes or No): _____

Action Step: _____

Complete(Yes or No): _____

Action Step: _____

Completed(Yes or No): _____

**Day 15**

Goal: _____

Action Step: _____

Completed(Yes or No): _____

Action Step: _____

Complete(Yes or No): _____

Action Step: _____

Completed(Yes or No): _____

**Day 16**

Goal: _____

Action Step: _____

Completed(Yes or No): _____

Action Step: _____

Complete(Yes or No): _____

Action Step: _____

Completed(Yes or No): _____

## Day 17

Goal: _____

Action Step: _____

Completed(Yes or No): _____


Action Step: _____

Complete(Yes or No): _____


Action Step: _____

Completed(Yes or No): _____


## Day 18

Goal: _____

Action Step: _____

Completed(Yes or No): _____


Action Step: _____

Complete(Yes or No): _____


Action Step: _____

Completed(Yes or No): _____

## Day 19

Goal: _____

Action Step: _____

Completed(Yes or No): _____


Action Step: _____

Complete(Yes or No): _____


Action Step: _____

Completed(Yes or No): _____


## Day 20

Goal: _____

Action Step: _____

Completed(Yes or No): _____


Action Step: _____

Complete(Yes or No): _____


Action Step: _____

Completed(Yes or No): _____

## Day 21

Goal: _____

Action Step: _____

Completed(Yes or No): _____

Action Step: _____

Complete(Yes or No): _____

Action Step: _____

Completed(Yes or No): _____

## Day 22

Goal: _____

Action Step: _____

Completed(Yes or No): _____

Action Step: _____

Complete(Yes or No): _____

Action Step: _____

Completed(Yes or No): _____

**Day 23**

Goal: _____

Action Step: _____

Completed(Yes or No): _____


Action Step: _____

Complete(Yes or No): _____


Action Step: _____

Completed(Yes or No): _____


**Day 24**

Goal: _____

Action Step: _____

Completed(Yes or No): _____


Action Step: _____

Complete(Yes or No): _____


Action Step: _____

Completed(Yes or No): _____

## Day 25

Goal: _____

Action Step: _____

Completed(Yes or No): _____

Action Step: _____

Complete(Yes or No): _____

Action Step: _____

Completed(Yes or No): _____

## Day 26

Goal: _____

Action Step: _____

Completed(Yes or No): _____

Action Step: _____

Complete(Yes or No): _____

Action Step: _____

Completed(Yes or No): _____

## Day 27

Goal: _____

Action Step: _____

Completed(Yes or No): _____


Action Step: _____

Complete(Yes or No): _____


Action Step: _____

Completed(Yes or No): _____


## Day 28

Goal: _____

Action Step: _____

Completed(Yes or No): _____


Action Step: _____

Complete(Yes or No): _____


Action Step: _____

Completed(Yes or No): _____

## Day 29

Goal: _____

Action Step: _____

Completed(Yes or No): _____

Action Step: _____

Complete(Yes or No): _____

Action Step: _____

Completed(Yes or No): _____

## Day 30

Goal: _____

Action Step: _____

Completed(Yes or No): _____

Action Step: _____

Complete(Yes or No): _____

Action Step: _____

Completed(Yes or No): _____

# Reference Page

"A.G. Gaston." *Think and Grow Rich: a Black Choice*, by Dennis Paul Kimbro and Napoleon Hill, Fawcett Columbine, 1997.

the Bees, Me and. "Our Sweet Story." *Me & the Bees Lemonade*, www.meandthebees.com/pages/about-us.

Davis, Scott. "Michael Jordan Once Added 15 Pounds of Muscle in One Summer to Prepare for a Rival and Changed the Way Athletes Train." *Insider*, Insider, 27 Apr. 2020, www.insider.com/michael-jordan-trained-15-pounds-muscle-pistons-2020-4#:~:text =Michael%20Jordan%20added%2015%20pounds,215%20with%20upper%2Dbody %20work.

The Editors of Encyclopaedia Britannica, The Editors of. "George Washington Carver." *Encyclopædia Britannica*, Encyclopædia Britannica, Inc., 24 July 2020, www.britannica.com/biography/George-Washington-Carver.

Loudenback, Tanza. "30 Celebrities Who Received Doctorate Degrees without Ever Stepping Foot in Class." *Business Insider*, Business Insider, 14 Sept. 2015, www.businessinsider.com/celebrities-who-have-honorary-degrees-2015-8#:~:text= Oprah%20Winfrey%20has%20four%20honorary%20doctorates.&text=The%20med ia%20mogul%20holds%20doctorates,%2C%20Duke%20University%2C%20and%2 0Harvard.

McKinney, Jeffrey. "45 Great Moments in Black Business – No. 24: A.G. Gaston Amasses $130 Million Fortune." *Black Enterprise*, Black Enterprise, 26 Mar. 2018, www.blackenterprise.com/45-great-moments-in-black-business-no-24-a-g-gaston-a masses-130-million-fortune/.

News, US. "Tuskegee University Overall Rankings | US News Best Colleges." *U.S. News & World Report*, U.S. News & World Report, 2020, www.usnews.com/best-colleges/tuskegee-university-1050/overall-rankings.

Online, Forbes. "America's Richest Self-Made Women 2019." *Forbes*, Forbes Magazine, 2019, www.forbes.com/self-made-women/#1b082acd6d96.

Papenfuss, Mary. "This 11-Year-Old Has Landed an $11 Million Deal with Whole Foods to Sell Her Homemade Lemonade." *Business Insider*, Business Insider, 31 Mar.2016, www.businessinsider.com/this-11-year-old-has-lands-whole-foods-to-sell-her-home made-lemonade-2016-3.

Washington, Booker T. *Up from Slavery*, 1901.

# Meet the Author

Darnell resides in Dallas, TX with his beautiful wife and awesome children: Delaya, Dallan, and Dara. In addition to being an author Darnell is a youth empowerment speaker. Darnell uses his engaging and interactive speaking style to help empower students to overcome obstacles and take ownership of their success and identify, and leverage their gift(s) to positively impact the world.

**Connect with Darnell:**

**Website: www.darnellspeaks.com**

**IG: @darnellspeaks**

**YouTube: @darnellSPEAKS**

*Thank you for reading this book. I know that you're a GONNABE and great success is in your future - Darnell*

Made in the USA
Middletown, DE
26 November 2023

43359972R00066